THE WORLD'S WORST NATURAL DISASTERS

T0060872

THE WORLD'S WORST
HURRICANES

by John R. Baker

CAPSTONE PRESS
a capstone imprint

Blazers Books are published by Capstone Press,
1710 Roe Crest Drive, North Mankato, Minnesota 56003
www.mycapstone.com

Library of Congress Cataloging-in-Publication Data
Names: Baker, John R. (John Ronald), 1989-
Title: The world's worst hurricanes / by John R. Baker.
Description: North Mankato, Minnesota: Capstone Press, 2017. | Series: Blazers.
  World's worst natural disasters| Audience: Grades 4 to 6. | Includes bibliographical
  references and index. | Description based on print version record and CIP data
  provided by publisher; resource not viewed.
Identifiers: LCCN 2016000605 (print) | LCCN 2015049416 (ebook) | ISBN
  9781515717973 (eBook PDF) | ISBN 9781515717898 (library binding) |
  ISBN 9781515717935 (paperback)
Subjects: LCSH: Hurricanes—History—Juvenile literature.
Classification: LCC QC944.2 (print) | LCC QC944.2 .B345 2017 (ebook) |
  DDC 551.55/209—dc23
LC record available at http://lccn.loc.gov/2016000605

Summary: Describes history's biggest and most
  destructive hurricanes from around the world.

Editorial Credits
Aaron Sautter, editor; Steve Mead, designer; Jo Miller,
media researcher; Tori Abraham, production specialist

Photo Credits
Alamy: Chronicle, 10–11; AP Images: Harry Koundakjian, 12–13;
Getty Images: The LIFE Picture Collection/Peter Stackpole, 22–
23; NASA: Earth Observatory, 26–27; Newscom: EPA/Vincent
Laforet, 16–17, Mirrorpix/Slater Arnold, 24–25, Reuters/Edgard
Garrido, 14–15; Reuters/Stringer/Philippines, 4–5, UPI/Chris
Carson, 28–29, ZUMA Press/Bill Gentile, 6–7, ZUMA Press/
Library of Congress, 8–9; NOAA, 18–19; Science Source, 20–21;
Shutterstock: leonello calvetti, cover, 3, 31; saphireleo, cover

Design Elements
Shutterstock: behindlens, xpixel

Printed in the United States   5824

TABLE OF CONTENTS

AWESOME POWER

HURRICANE CATEGORIES

5
4
3
2
1

A hurricane's strength is based on its wind speed. Hurricanes are ranked on a scale from 1 to 5. Category 5 hurricanes are the most powerful storms in the world.

Huge ocean waves pound the shore. Ferocious winds hammer buildings and uproot trees. A hurricane's power is an awesome sight. Nature's most powerful storms bring destruction around the world every year. Read on to learn about the worst hurricanes ever seen.

CATEGORY

1	2	3	4	5
74 to 95 mph (119 to 153 kph)	96 to 110 mph (154 to 177 kph)	111 to 130 mph (178 to 209 kph)	131 to 155 mph (210 to 249 kph)	156+ mph (250+ kph)

Wind Speeds (miles/kilometers per hour)

HURRICANE ANDREW

Location:
Florida, Louisiana, Bahamas

Date:
August 16–28, 1992

5
4
3
2
1

Hurricane Andrew slammed into Florida on August 24, 1992. Its winds reached 165 miles (266 km) per hour. The Category 5 storm was incredibly destructive. It toppled trees and crushed whole neighborhoods.

FACT Hurricane Andrew was one of the costliest storms in history. It did $26.5 billion in damage in the United States alone.

DISASTER IN GALVESTON

Location:
Galveston, Texas

Date:
August 27–
September 8, 1900

5
4
3
2
1

Galveston, Texas, was a booming city in 1900. Then a powerful hurricane hit. The storm created a massive 15.5-foot (4.7-meter) **storm surge**. It pushed a wall of **debris** across the city. Few buildings were left standing.

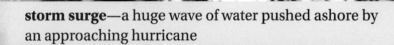

storm surge—a huge wave of water pushed ashore by an approaching hurricane

The Galveston hurricane was the deadliest natural disaster in U.S. history. The storm killed between 6,000 and 12,000 people.

debris—the scattered pieces of something that has been broken or destroyed

THE GREAT HURRICANE OF 1780

Location:
Caribbean Sea

Date:
October 9–20,
1780

5
4
3
2
1

The Great Hurricane of 1780 may have
affected the Revolutionary War (1775–1783).
The storm destroyed most of the British
ships in the Caribbean Sea. This may have
helped America win its **independence**.

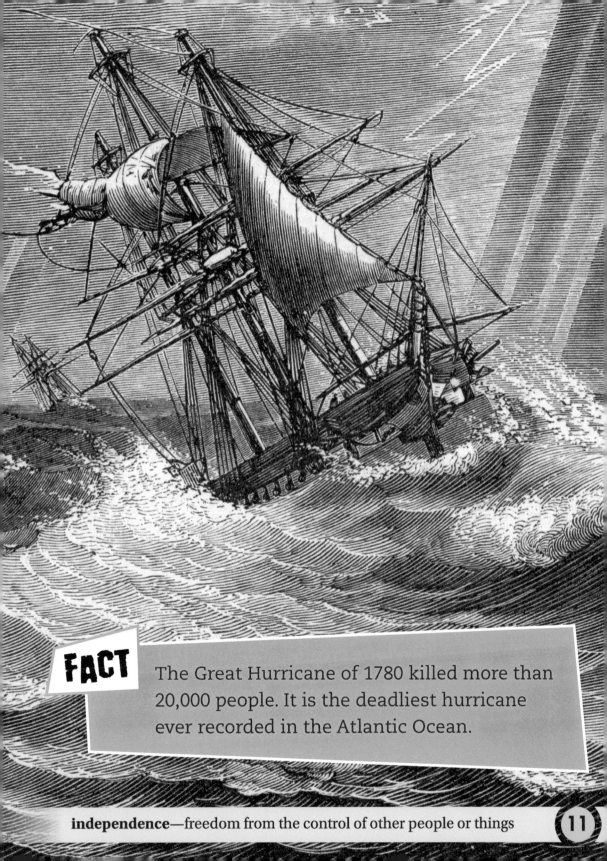

FACT The Great Hurricane of 1780 killed more than 20,000 people. It is the deadliest hurricane ever recorded in the Atlantic Ocean.

independence—freedom from the control of other people or things

HISTORY'S DEADLIEST STORM

Location:
Bhola, Bangladesh

Date:
November 7–13, 1970

Bhola, Bangladesh, was hit by history's deadliest storm in 1970. The powerful **cyclone** created a 20-foot- (6.1-m-) high storm surge. It swept away homes, trees, animals, and people. Up to 500,000 people died in the disaster.

cyclone—a storm with strong winds that blow around a central point

A RECORD-SETTING STORM

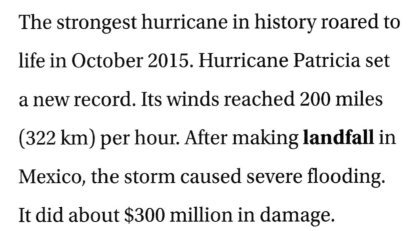

Location:
southwestern
Mexico

Date:
October 20–24,
2015

5
4
3
2
1

The strongest hurricane in history roared to life in October 2015. Hurricane Patricia set a new record. Its winds reached 200 miles (322 km) per hour. After making **landfall** in Mexico, the storm caused severe flooding. It did about $300 million in damage.

landfall—the area where a hurricane moves over land

Hurricane Patricia weakened very quickly after hitting land. It dropped from a Category 5 storm to a **remnant low** in less than 24 hours.

remnant low—the remains of a hurricane with winds less than 39 miles (63 km) per hour

HURRICANE KATRINA

Location:
southeastern
United States

Date:
August 23–30,
2005

Hurricane Katrina was one of the worst disasters in U.S. history. It slammed into the Gulf Coast with winds of 120 miles (193 km) per hour. It brought a storm surge that overwhelmed **levees** in New Orleans, Louisiana. Most of the city was flooded.

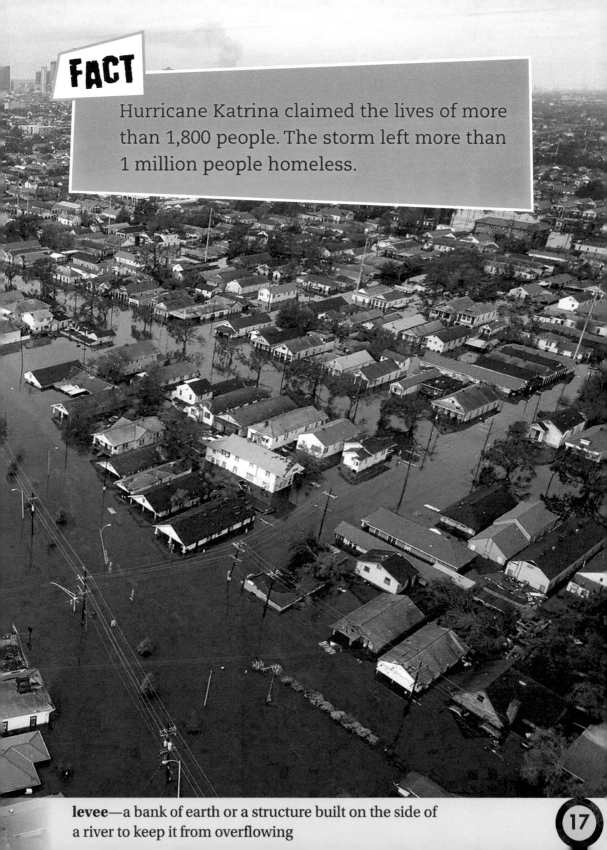

FACT

Hurricane Katrina claimed the lives of more than 1,800 people. The storm left more than 1 million people homeless.

levee—a bank of earth or a structure built on the side of a river to keep it from overflowing

HURRICANE CAMILLE

Location:
southeast United States, Cuba

Date:
August 14–22, 1969

5
4
3
2
1

Hurricane Camille roared into the Gulf Coast in August 1969. The storm brought winds close to 200 miles (322 km) per hour. It also dumped up to 31 inches (79 centimeters) of rain. Camille caused close to $1.4 billion of destruction across the southeastern United States.

FACT

Hurricane Camille created a 25-foot (7.6-m) storm surge that left large ships stranded on beaches.

1935 LABOR DAY HURRICANE

Location:
Florida Keys,
Florida

Date:
August 29–
September 10, 1935

The 1935 Labor Day Hurricane devastated the Florida Keys. The storm's winds reached 185 miles (298 km) per hour. A huge storm surge pushed over a train. A ship was blown more than 3 miles (4.8 km) **inland**.

FACT

The 1935 Labor Day Hurricane claimed the lives of more than 400 people.

inland—away from the ocean

HURRICANE DONNA

Location:
Puerto Rico, Cuba, Bahamas, eastern United States

Date:
August 29–
September 13, 1960

Rating:

5
4
3
2
1

In 1960 Hurricane Donna was one long-lived storm. It first hit the Florida Keys. Then it turned northeast to pound North Carolina. It next hit Rhode Island with 130 mile (209 km) per hour winds. The storm finally **dissipated** over Canada.

FACT

Hurricane Donna traveled more than 2,000 miles (3,219 km).

dissipate—to break apart and disappear

MIGHTY MITCH

Location:
Central America

Date:
October 22–
November 5, 1998

Hurricane Mitch hit Central America in 1998. The storm dumped more than 6 feet (1.8 m) of rain on Honduras and Nicaragua. The water rushed down the mountains. **Mudslides** wiped out entire villages.

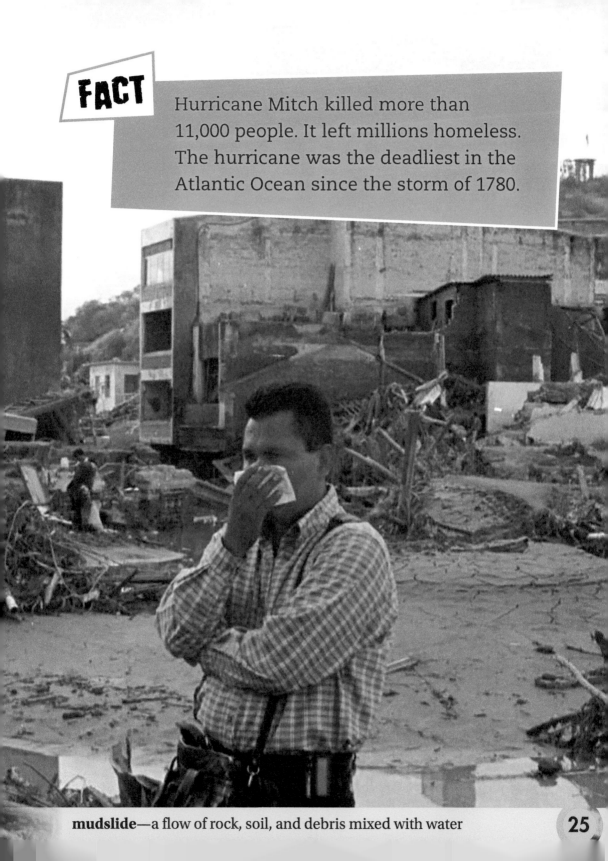

Hurricane Mitch killed more than 11,000 people. It left millions homeless. The hurricane was the deadliest in the Atlantic Ocean since the storm of 1780.

mudslide—a flow of rock, soil, and debris mixed with water

SUPERSTORM SANDY

Location:
Jamaica, Cuba, Northeast United States

Date:
October 22–31, 2012

In 2012 Hurricane Sandy became the second costliest storm in U.S. history. It washed away beaches. It flooded entire cities. Thousands of homes were destroyed. Sandy caused the deaths of more than 200 people. It caused nearly $75 billion in damage.

FACT

Because of its size, Hurricane Sandy is often called "Superstorm Sandy." At one point the monster storm's winds stretched more than 940 miles (1,513 km) wide.

SURVIVING HURRICANES

In case of a hurricane warning, be prepared. Board up windows. Stock up on food and water. Be ready to **evacuate** if necessary. Hurricanes are dangerous storms. People must respect their power and take steps to stay safe.

DISASTER EMERGENCY KIT

An emergency kit can be very helpful in case of a hurricane. A good kit should include these items:

- ✔ first-aid kit
- ✔ flashlight
- ✔ battery-powered radio
- ✔ extra batteries
- ✔ blankets
- ✔ bottled water
- ✔ canned and dried food
- ✔ can opener
- ✔ whistle to alert rescue workers

evacuate—to leave a dangerous place and go somewhere safer

GLOSSARY

cyclone (SY-clohn)—a storm with strong winds that blow around a central point

debris (duh-BREE)—the scattered pieces of something that has been broken or destroyed

dissipate (DISS-ih-payt)—to break apart and disappear

evacuate (i-VA-kyuh-wayt)—to leave a dangerous place and go somewhere safer

independence (in-di-PEN-duhnss)—freedom from the control of other people or things

inland (IN-luhnd)—away from the ocean

landfall (LAND-fawl)—the area where a hurricane moves over land

levee (LEV-ee)—a bank of earth or a structure built on the side of a river to keep it from overflowing

mudslide (MUHD-slide)—a flow of rock, earth, and debris mixed with water

remnant low (REM-nuhnt LOW)—the remains of a hurricane with winds less than 39 miles (63 km) per hour

storm surge (STORM SURJ)—a huge wave of water pushed ashore by an approaching hurricane

READ MORE

Challoner, Jack. *Eyewitness Hurricane & Tornado*. DK Eyewitness. New York: DK Publishing, 2014.

Gray-Wilburn, Renée. *Hurricanes: Be Aware and Prepare*. Weather Aware. North Mankato, Minn.: Capstone Press, 2015.

Raum, Elizabeth. *Surviving Hurricanes*. Children's True Stories: Natural Disasters. Chicago: Raintree, 2012.

INTERNET SITES

Facthound offers a safe, fun way to find Internet sites related to this book. All of the sites on Facthound have been researched by our staff.

Here's all you do:
Visit *www.facthound.com*
Type in this code: 9781515717898

Check out projects, games and lots more at
www.capstonekids.com

CRITICAL THINKING USING THE COMMON CORE

1. Hurricanes are the most powerful and deadliest storms in the world. Which hurricane killed the most people in history? Which one caused the most damage? (Key Ideas and Details)

2. Explain what you should do if a hurricane warning is issued for your area. (Craft and Structure)

3. Look at the chart on pages 4–5. What are the wind speeds for each category of hurricane? (Integration of Knowledge and Ideas)

INDEX